GIRLS' SONGS FROM 21ST CENTURY MUSICALS
10 SONGS FROM SHOWS SINCE 2000

To access companion recorded accompaniments online, visit:
www.halleonard.com/mylibrary

Enter Code
7604-3287-9027-9120

ISBN 978-1-5400-4334-4

Visit Hal Leonard Online at
www.halleonard.com

Contact us:
Hal Leonard
7777 West Bluemound Road
Milwaukee, WI 53213
Email: info@halleonard.com

In Europe, contact:
Hal Leonard Europe Limited
42 Wigmore Street
Marylebone, London, W1U 2RN
Email: info@halleonardeurope.com

In Australia, contact:
Hal Leonard Australia Pty. Ltd.
4 Lentara Court
Cheltenham, Victoria, 3192 Australia
Email: info@halleonard.com.au

CONTENTS
ALPHABETICALLY BY SHOW

Pianists on the recordings: [1] Brendan Fox, [2] Richard Walters

CONTENTS
ALPHABETICALLY BY SONG

Pianists on the recordings: [1] Brendan Fox, [2] Richard Walters

The price of this publications includes access to companion recorded accompaniments online, for download or streaming, using the unique code found on the title page. Visit **www.halleonard.com/mylibrary** and enter the access code.

DO YOU WANT TO BUILD A SNOWMAN?

from *Frozen*

Music and Lyrics by Kristen Anderson-Lopez
and Robert Lopez

an - y - more.   Come out the door!   It's like you've gone a - way.

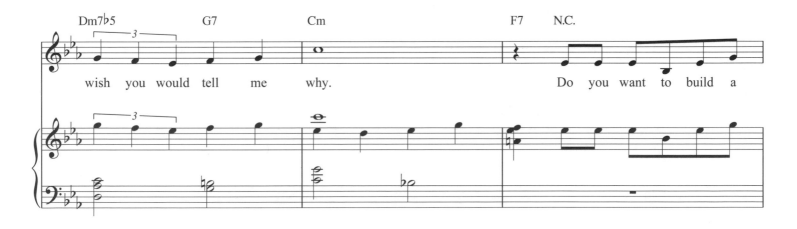

We used to be best bud - dies,   and now we're not. ___   I

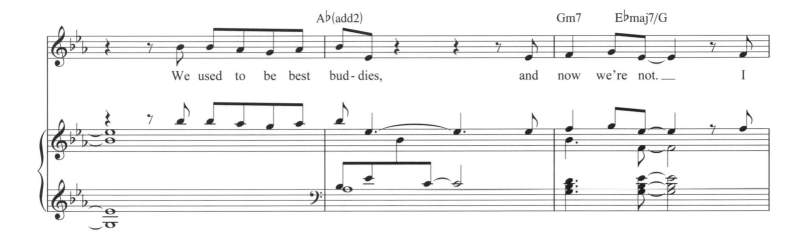

wish you would tell me why.   Do you want to build a

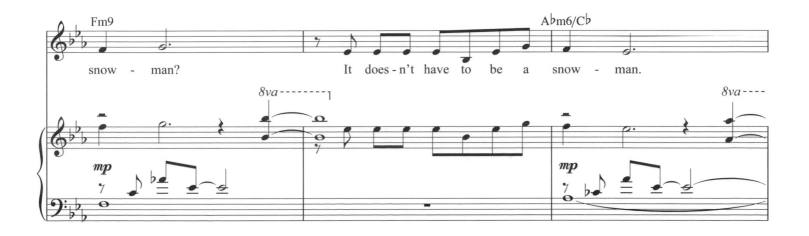

snow - man?   It does - n't have to be a snow - man.

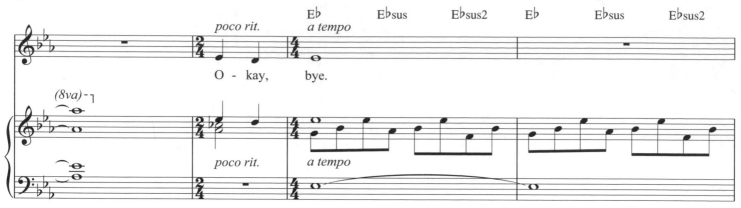

O - kay, bye.

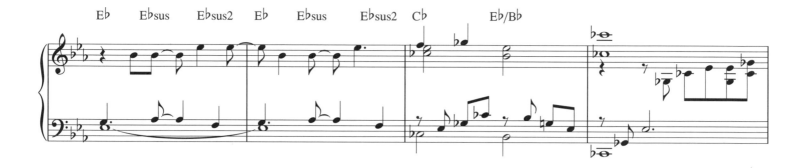

A little faster

Do you want to build a snow - man? Or ride our bikes a - round the

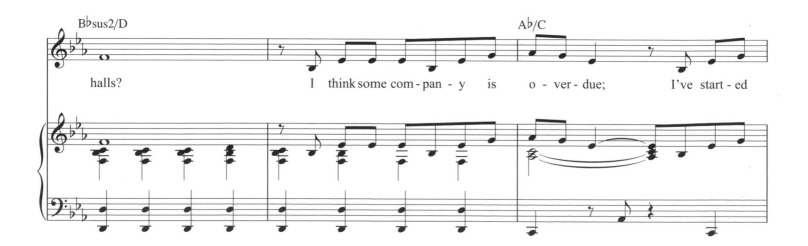

halls? I think some com - pan - y is o - ver - due; I've start - ed

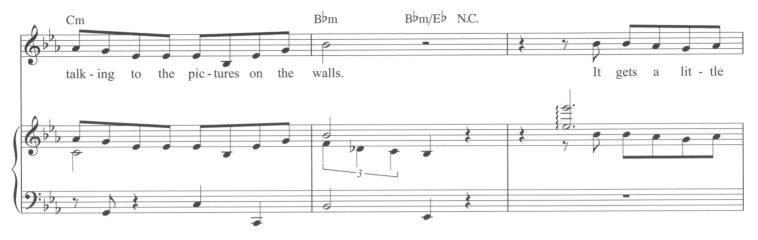

talk - ing to the pic - tures on the walls.　　　It gets a lit - tle

lone - ly,　　all these emp - ty __ rooms, _　just watch - ing the hours tick

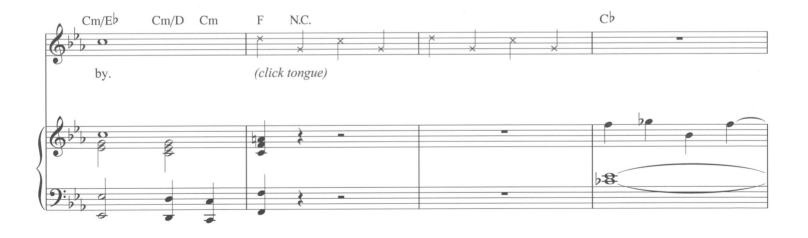

by.　　　　(click tongue)

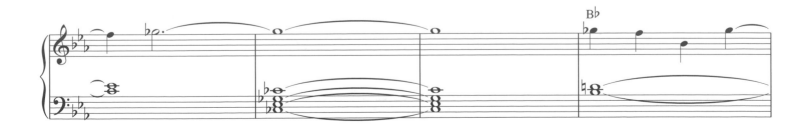

N.C.

(knocking)   (Spoken:) Elsa?

A little slower, tenderly

E♭sus2

(Sung:) Please,   I know you're   in   there.   Peo - ple   are   ask - ing   where you've

p

3

B♭sus2/D

A♭/C

been.   They say, "Have cour - age,"   and I'm   try - ing   to;   I'm right   out

Cm   Gm   G(sus2/4)   Gm

here   for   you,   just   let   me   in.   We   on - ly   have   each

oth - er; it's just you and me. ___ What are we gon - na

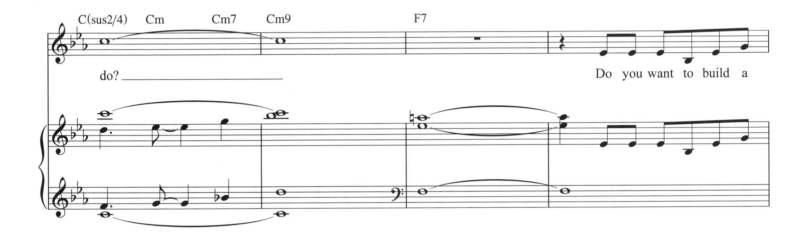

do? ___ Do you want to build a

Slower

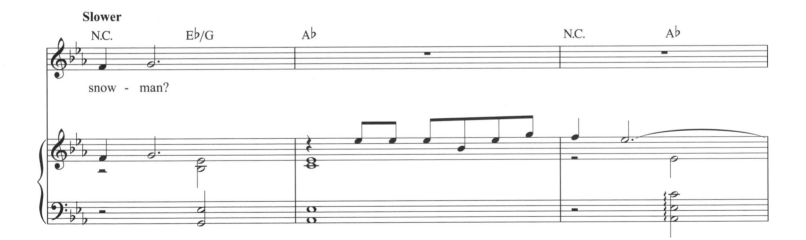

snow - man?

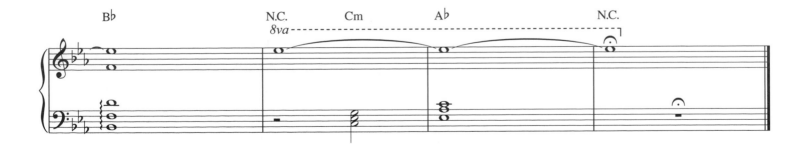

A LITTLE BIT OF YOU

from *Frozen: The Broadway Musical*

Music and Lyrics by Kristen Anderson-Lopez
and Robert Lopez

This duet has been adapted as a solo.

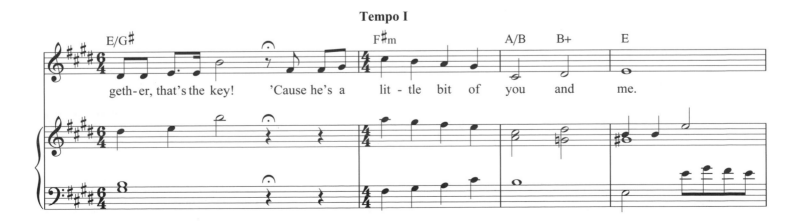

La la la la la la la la la la la la la la la la

la la la la.

Faster yet (♩ = 176)

Lit - tle bit of you. ____

Lit - tle bit of

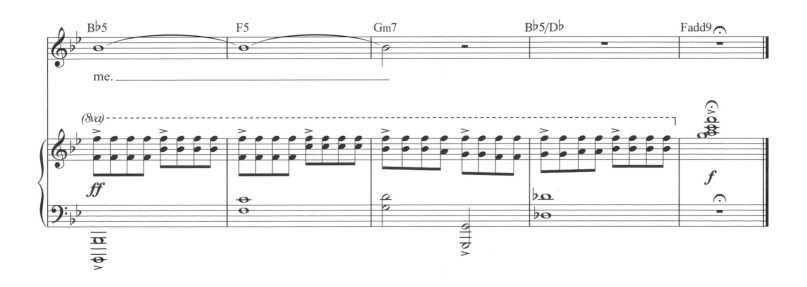

me. ____

PART OF YOUR WORLD

from *The Little Mermaid - A Broadway Musical*

Music by Alan Menken
Lyrics by Howard Ashman

Simply, in 2

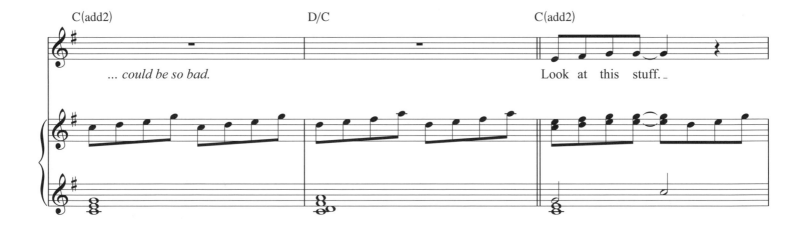

Would-n't you think _ I'm the girl, ___ the girl who has ev - 'ry - thing?

Look at this trove, _ treas-ures un - told. _

How man - y won - ders can one cav - ern hold? Look-ing a - round _ here you'd think, _

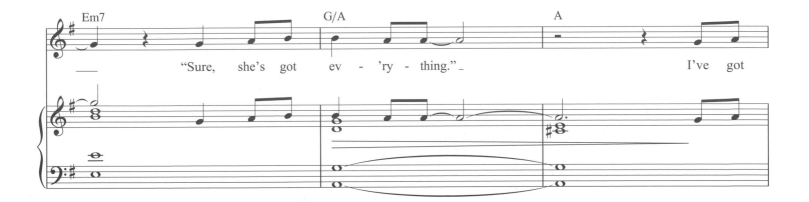

_ "Sure, she's got ev - 'ry - thing." _ I've got

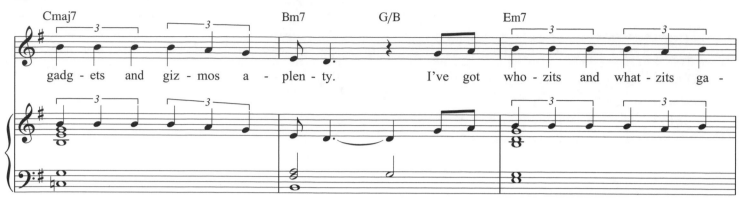

gadg - ets and giz - mos a - plen - ty. I've got who - zits and what - zits ga -

lore. You want thing - a - ma - bobs? I've got twen - ty. But who

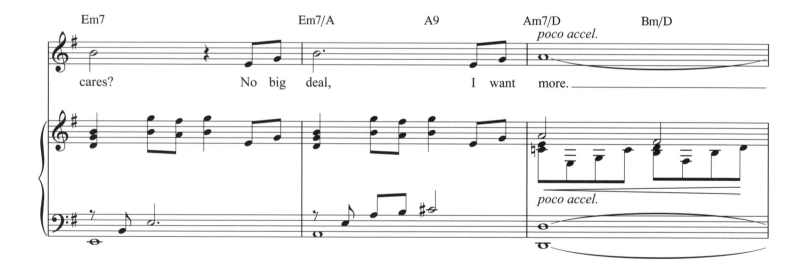

cares? No big deal, I want more. _____

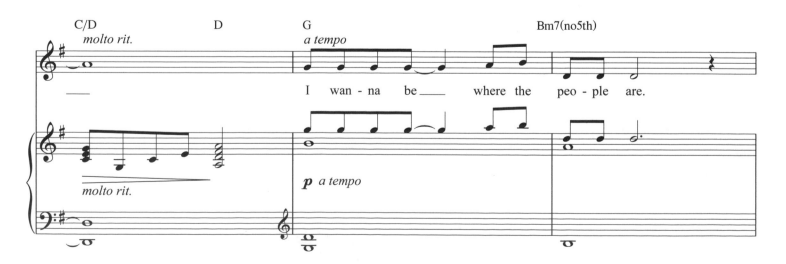

I wan - na be _____ where the peo - ple are.

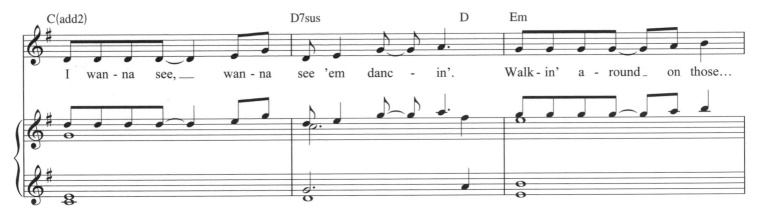

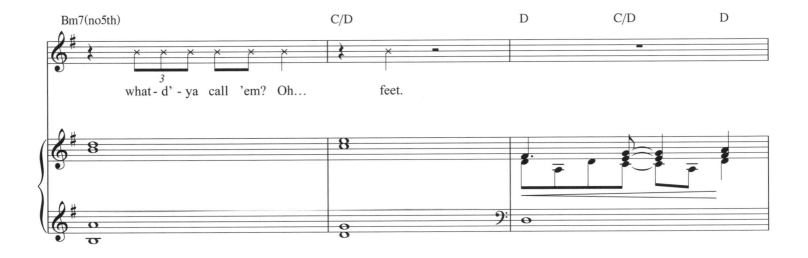

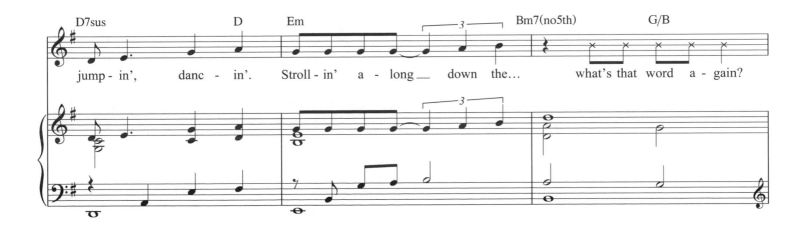

18

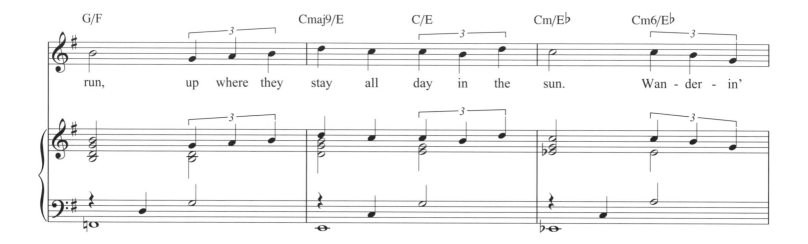

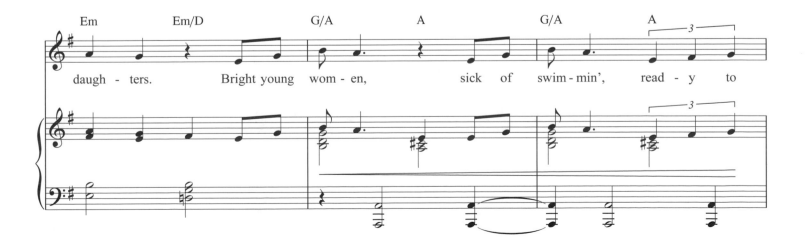

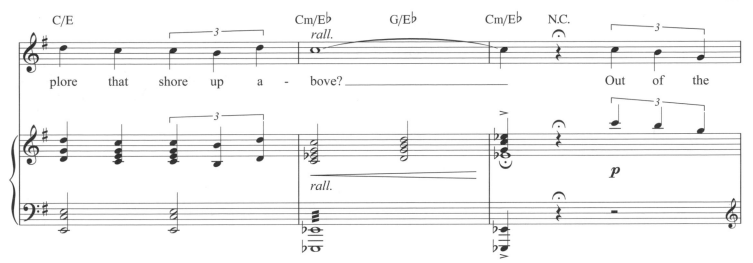

plore that shore up a - bove? _____ Out of the

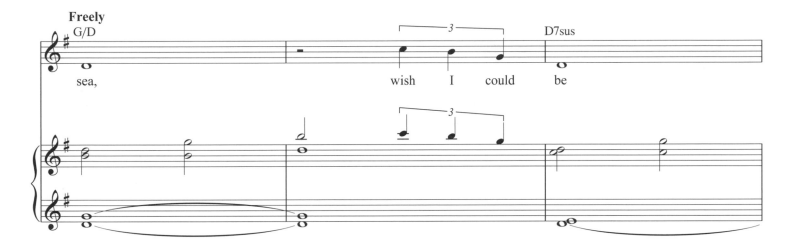

sea, wish I could be

part of that world. _____

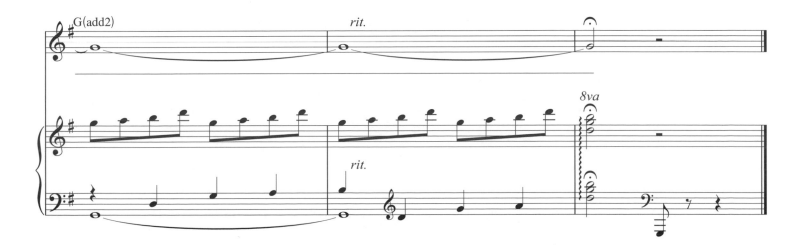

HALFWAY
from *Amélie*

Lyrics by Nathan Tysen and Daniel Messé
Music by Daniel Messé

This duet has beeen adapted as a solo.

She taught a les-son a-bout___ a boat___ that is sail - ing the sea,___

try - ing to get___ from point A to B. So the

lit - tle boat's trav - el - ing at___ full sail,___ and it's try - ing to reach___ the shore.___

But when - ev - er the boat___ gets half - way there,___ there is

al - ways half - way more. ___ You take half of half ___ and

half of that, ___ so ___ on and on ___ and so... ___

poco cresc.

In my moth - er's school - house, ___ there was

al - ways half - way to go. ___

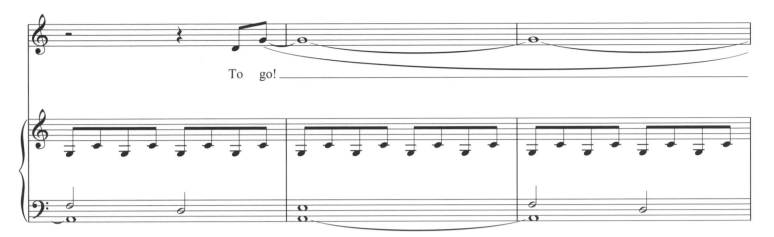

To go!

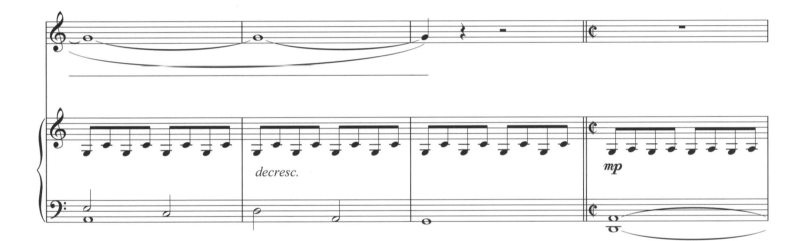

decresc.   mp

Lit-tle boat, big o - cean._____   Lit-tle boat,_ big o -

mf

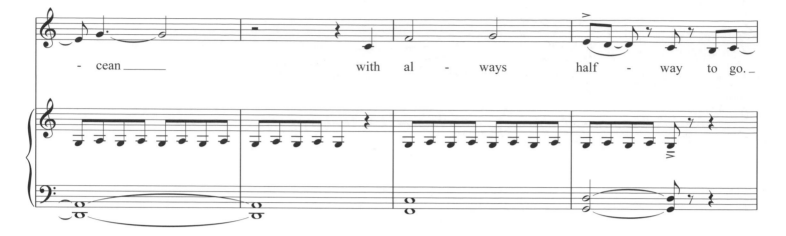

-cean _____ with al - ways half - way to go. _

To go! _____

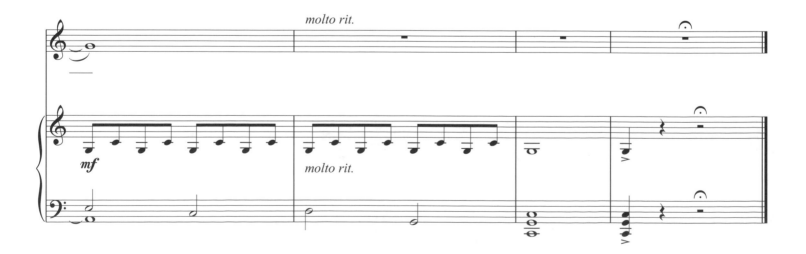

molto rit.

NAUGHTY
from *Matilda the Musical*

Words and Music by
Tim Minchin

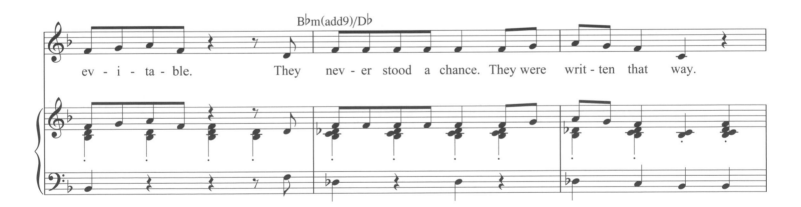

Ro - me - o and Ju - li - et: 'twas writ - ten in the stars be - fore they e - ven met

that love and fate and a touch of stu - pid - i - ty would

rob them of their hope of liv - ing hap - pi - ly. The end - ings are of - ten a

lit - tle bit go - ry. *(Finger snaps)* I won - der why they did - n't just change their sto - ry.

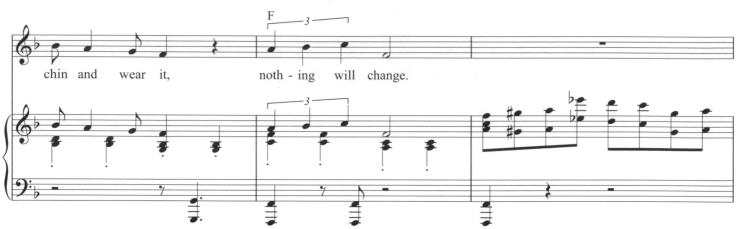

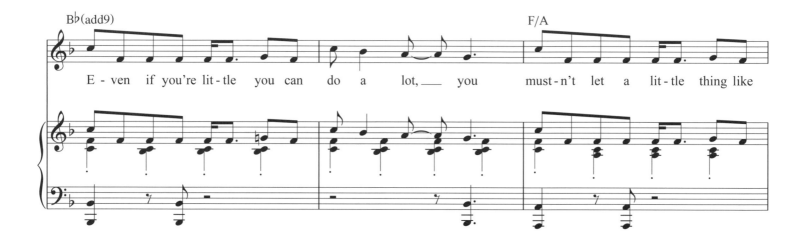

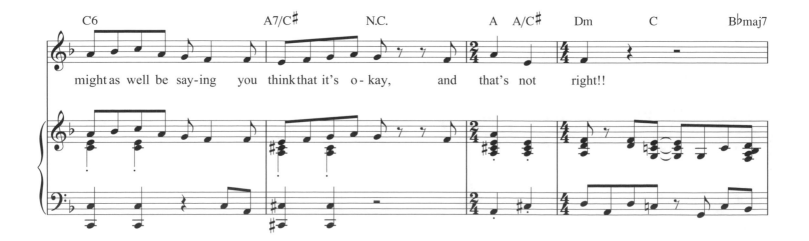

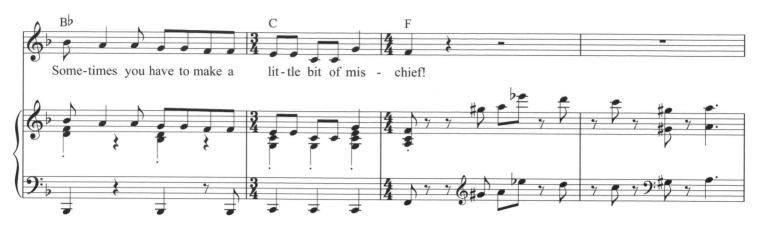

Some-times you have to make a lit-tle bit of mis - chief!

Just be-cause you find that life's _

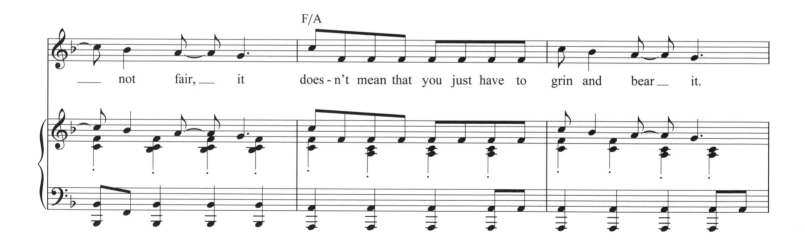

_ not fair, _ it does-n't mean that you just have to grin and bear _ it.

If you al-ways take it on the chin and wear it, noth - ing will change.

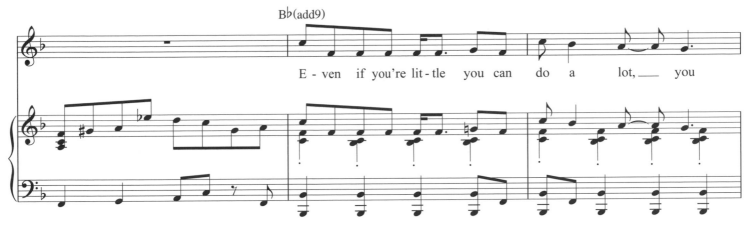

E - ven if you're lit - tle you can do a lot, ___ you

must-n't let a lit-tle thing like lit-tle stop ___ you. If you sit a - round and let them

get on top, ___ you might as well be say - ing you think that it's o - kay, and

that's not right! And if it's not right,

you have to put it right.

In the slip of a bolt, there's a ti - ny re - volt. The see of a war

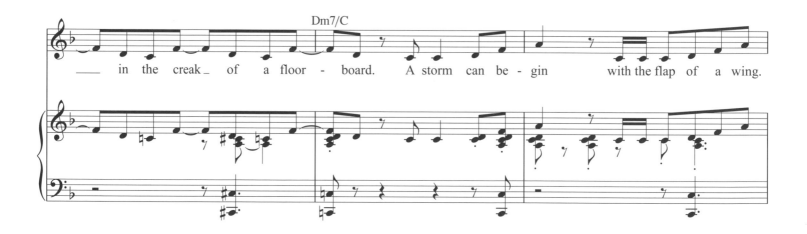

— in the creak of a floor - board. A storm can be - gin with the flap of a wing.

The ti - ni - est mite packs the might - i - est sting. Ev - 'ry day

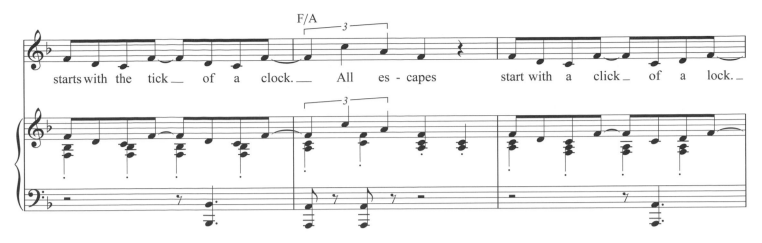

starts with the tick __ of a clock. __ All es - capes start with a click __ of a lock. __

__ If you're stuck __ in your sto - ry and want to get out, __ you don't have to cry, __

__ you don't have to shout! __ 'Cause if you're lit - tle, you can do a lot, __ you must -

- n't let a lit - tle thing like lit - tle stop __ you. If you sit a - round and let them

get on top, ___ you won't change a thing.

Just be-cause you find that life's not fair, it does-n't mean that you just have to

grin and bear __ it. If you al-ways take it on the chin and wear it, you

might as well be say-ing you think that it's o-kay, and that's not right!

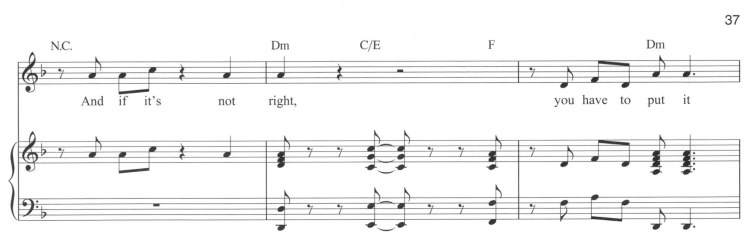

And if it's not right, you have to put it

right. But no-bod-y else __ is gon-na

put it right for me. No-bod-y but me is gon-na change my sto-ry.

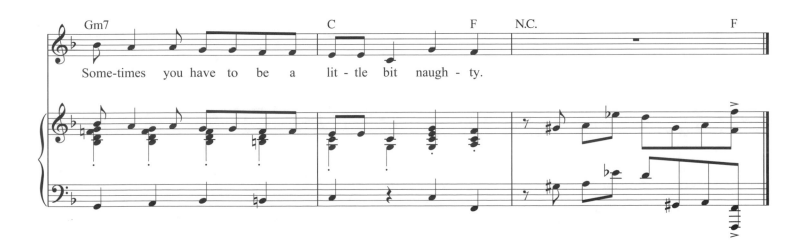

Some-times you have to be a lit-tle bit naugh-ty.

QUIET
from *Matilda the Musical*

Words and Music by
Tim Minchin

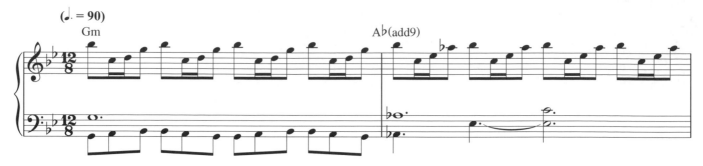

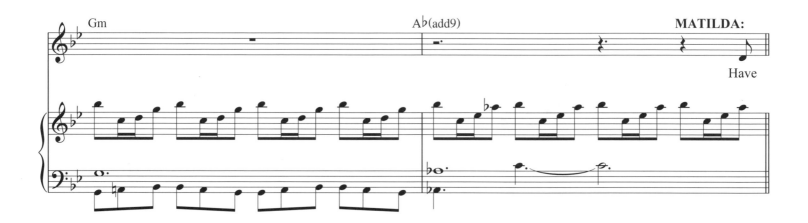

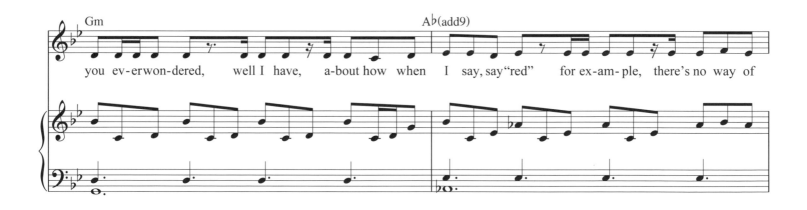

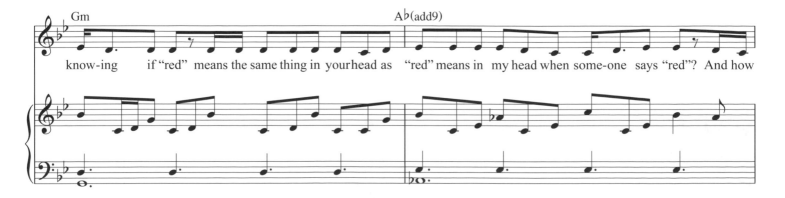

if we are trav-el-ing at al-most the speed of light and we're hold-ing a light, that light would still

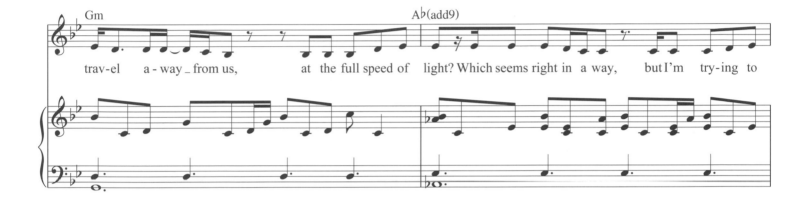

trav-el a - way _ from us, at the full speed of light? Which seems right in a way, but I'm try-ing to

say, I'm not sure, but I won-der if in - side my head, I'm not just a bit dif-f'rent from some of my

friends. These an-swers that come in - to my mind un - bid-den. These stor-ies de - liv-ered to me ful - ly

writ-ten. And when ev-'ry one shouts like they seem to like shout-ing, the noise in my head is in-cred-i - bly loud

and I just wish they'd stop, my dad and my mum, and the tel-ly and stor-ies would stop for just

once. And I'm sor-ry I'm not quite ex-plain-ing it right, _ but this noise be-comes an - ger, and the an-ger is

light, and this burn-ing in-side me would us-ual-ly fade, _ but it is-n't to day, _ and the heat and the

shout- ing, and my heart is pound-ing and my eyes are burn- ing, and sud-den - ly

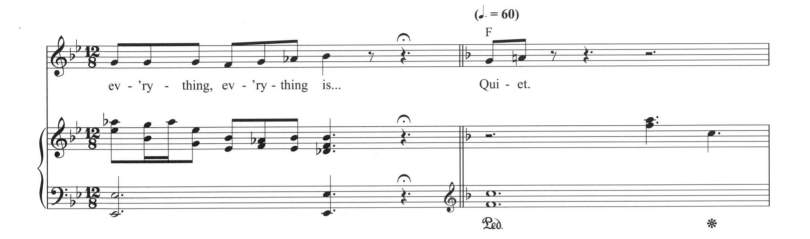

(♩. = 60)

ev - 'ry - thing, ev - 'ry-thing is... Qui - et.

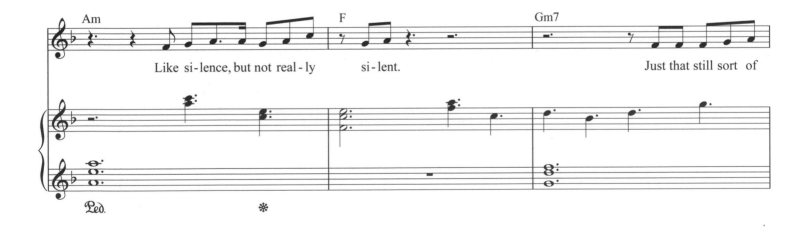

Like si-lence, but not real - ly si - lent. Just that still sort of

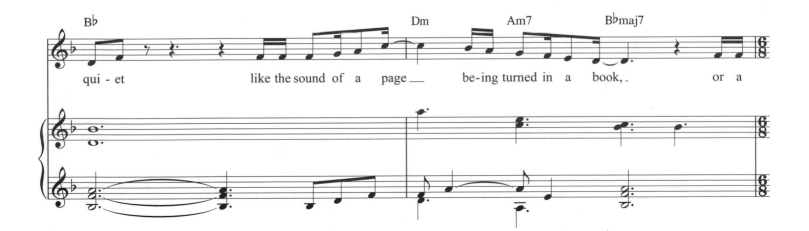

qui - et like the sound of a page be-ing turned in a book, or a

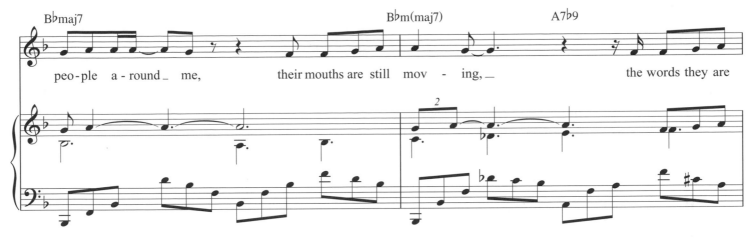

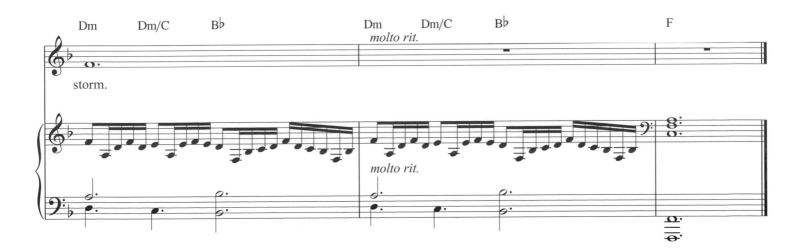

I KNOW IT'S TODAY
from *Shrek the Musical*

Words and Music by David Lindsey-Abaire
and Jeanine Tesori

The first verse is sung by Young Fiona, presented here. Then Teen Fiona and the adult Fiona take over.

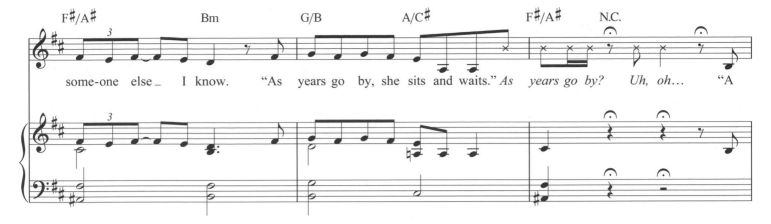

some-one else _ I know. "As years go by, she sits and waits." *As years go by? Uh, oh…* "A

tor - tur - ous _ ex - is - tence." *I don't re-mem - ber this part.* "She wish-es she were dead." *Skip a -*

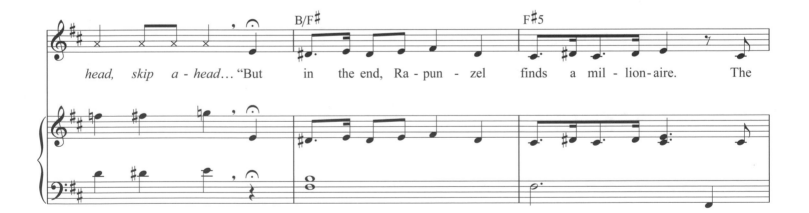

head, skip a - head… "But in the end, Ra - pun - zel finds a mil - lion-aire. The

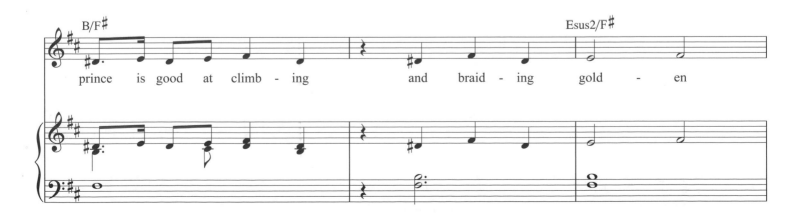

prince is good at climb - ing and braid - ing gold - en

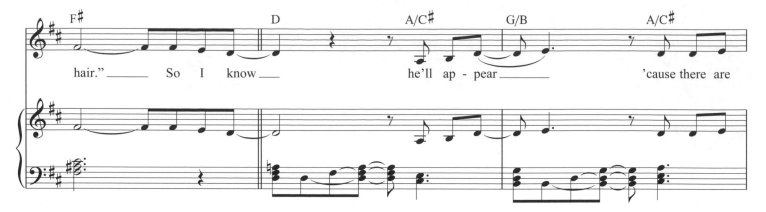

hair." ___ So I know ___ he'll ap - pear ___ 'cause there are

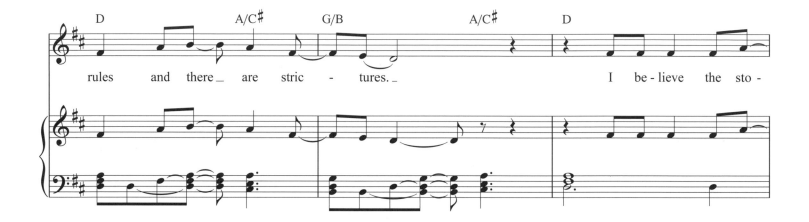

rules and there __ are stric - tures. __ I be - lieve the sto -

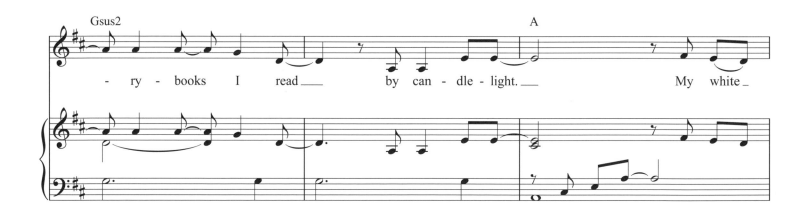

- ry - books I read ___ by can - dle - light. ___ My white __

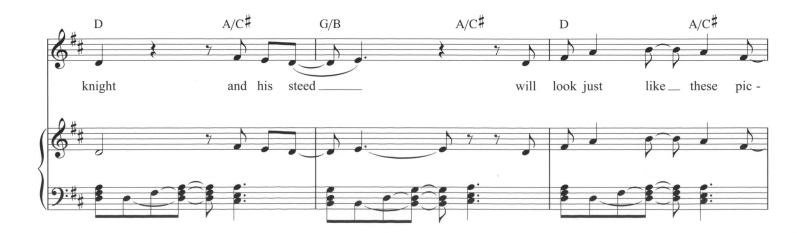

knight and his steed ___ will look just like __ these pic -

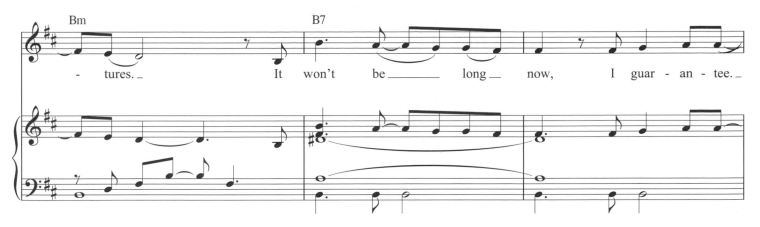

It won't be ____ long ____ now, I guar - an - tee. ____

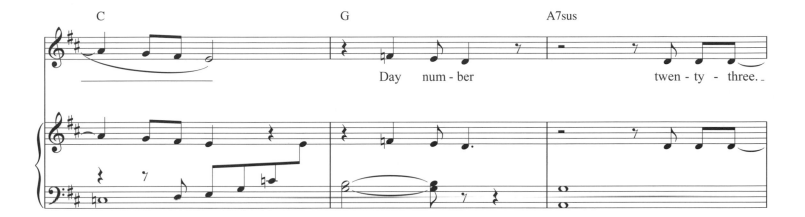

Day num - ber ____ twen - ty - three. ____

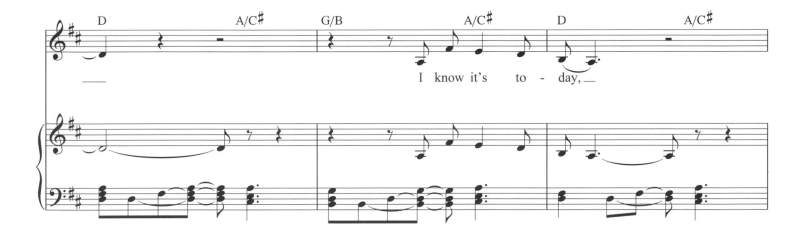

I know it's to - day, ____

I know it's to - day. _____

HOME
from the Broadway Musical *Wonderland*

Music by Frank Wildhorn
Lyrics by Jack Murphy

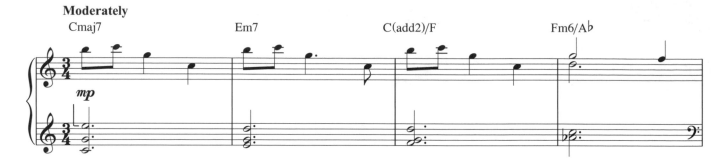

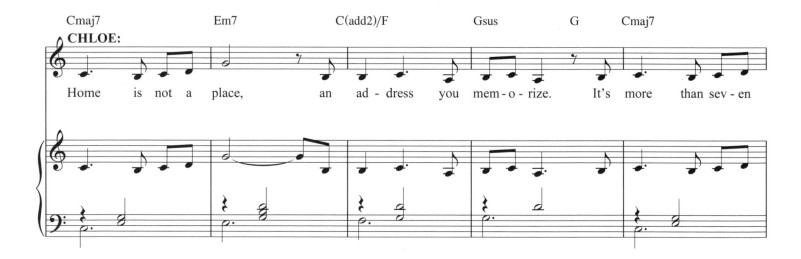

CHLOE:
Home is not a place, an ad-dress you mem-o-rize. It's more than sev-en

flights or a-part-ment 8 - A. It's where you nev-er feel lone-ly when-

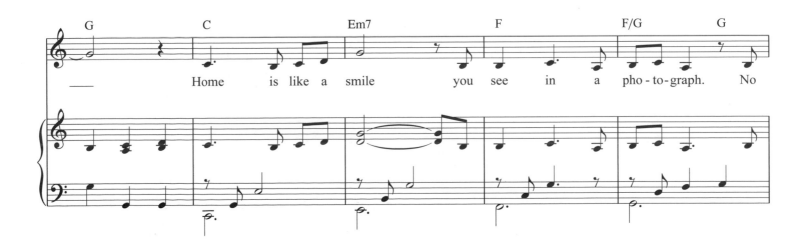

mat - ter what you do, it's not sup-posed to change. Why can't we

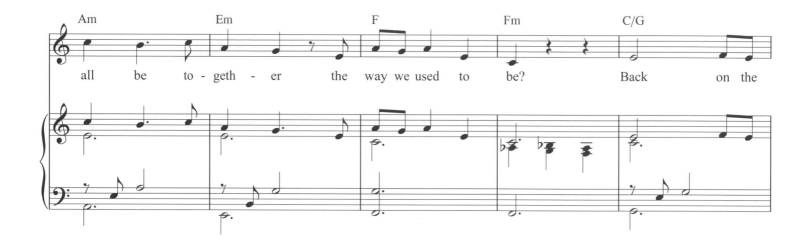

all be to-geth - er the way we used to be? Back on the

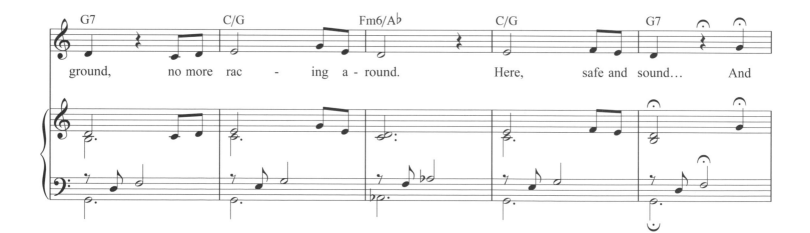

ground, no more rac - ing a - round. Here, safe and sound... And

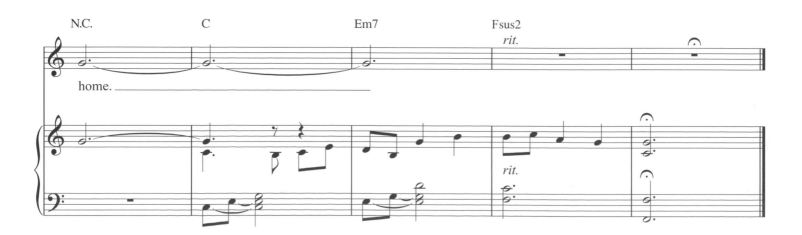

home.

EVERLASTING
from *Tuck Everlasting*

Music by Chris Miller
Lyrics by Nathan Tysen

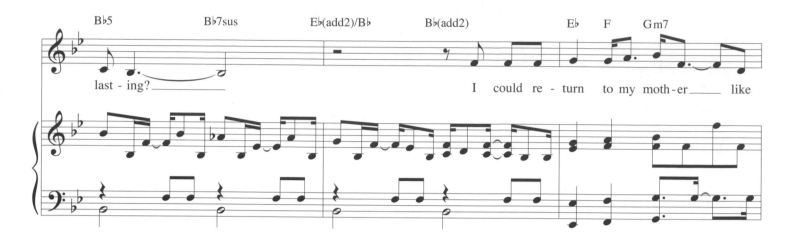

last - ing?_____

I could re - turn to my moth-er_____ like

noth-ing_____ has hap-pened._____ Live like an im - pos - ter for six long years.

Turn sev - en - teen, then good girl Win-nie Fos - ter_____

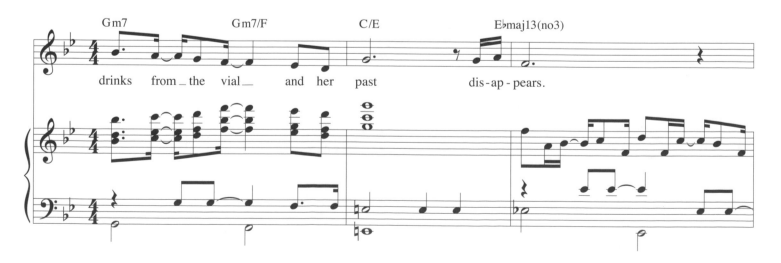

drinks from __ the vial __ and her past dis - ap - pears.

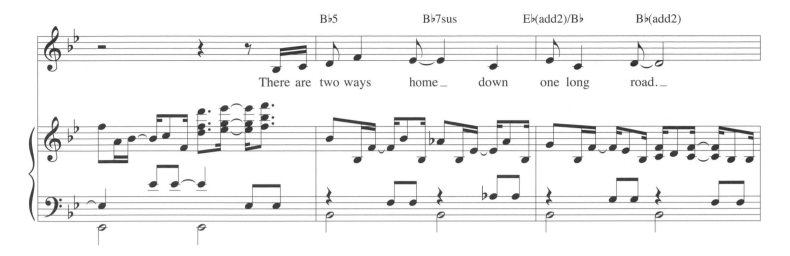

There are two ways home_ down one long road._

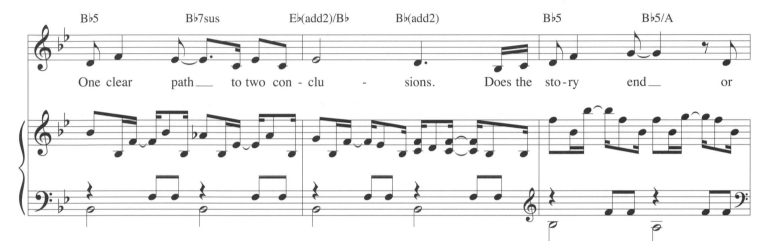

One clear path_ to two con - clu - sions. Does the sto-ry end_ or

nev - er_ end?_ Does the se - cret fade,_____ or is it ev-er-

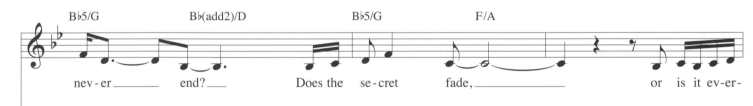

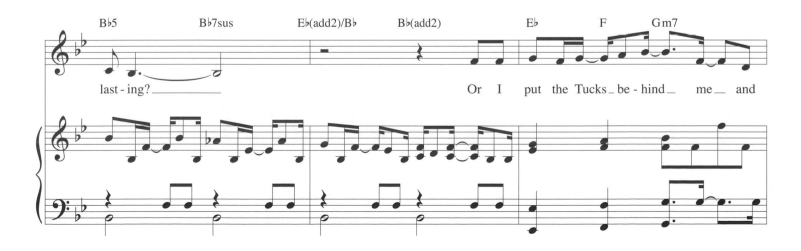

last - ing?_____ Or I put the Tucks_ be - hind_ me_ and

pull up__ the an - chor.__ Ride the wheel_ plen-ty____ for all that it's__ worth._

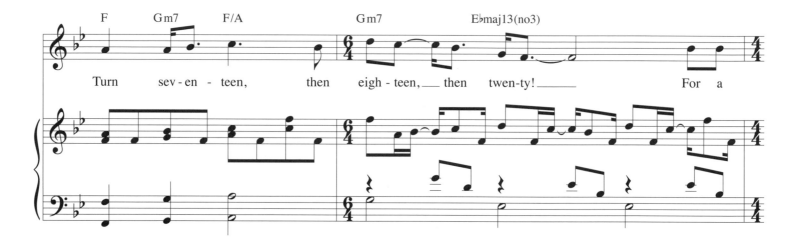

Turn sev - en - teen, then eigh - teen,__ then twen-ty!____ For a

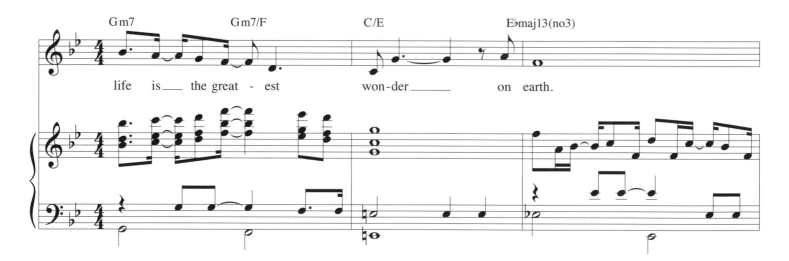

life is__ the great - est won-der____ on earth.

Can I,__ should I,__ do I__ drink?

GOOD GIRL WINNIE FOSTER
from *Tuck Everlasting*

Music by Chris Miller
Lyrics by Nathan Tysen

fly the coop if on-ly I could._____ But I've got a

real-ly bad case of be-ing good. I'd

go find trou-ble if there was some to get in. Ask a

friend to play if I had one to let in._____ Na - na's

rock - er saw - ing through the floor, ev - 'ry day just like the one be - fore. We

lock our - selves be - hind that door. _____ Is it

wrong to wish for some - thing more? _____

Good girl Win - nie Fos - ter ev - 'ry day

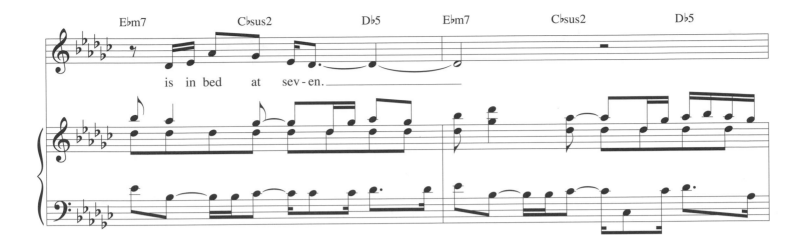

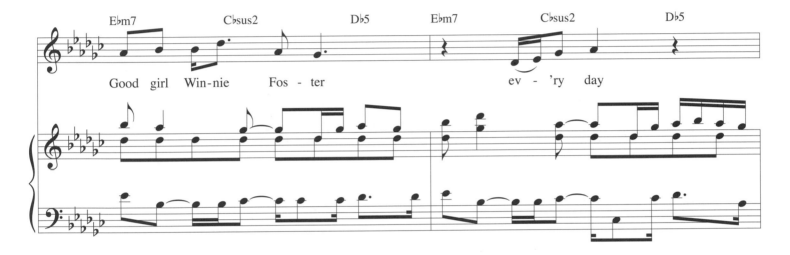

60

a lit-tle some-thing more than

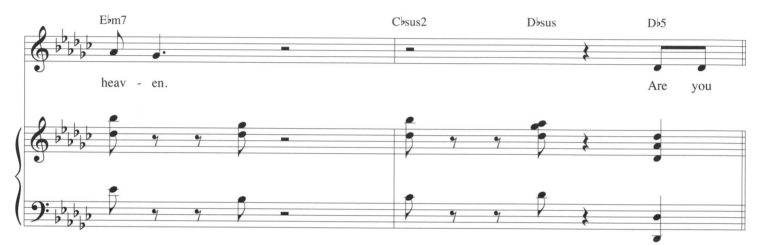

heav - en. Are you

from the wood? I'm not al-lowed there._____ Big

news, I know, I'm not al-lowed an-y-where. Well

now's your chance to dis-ap-pear. Go have fun, I'll be right here.

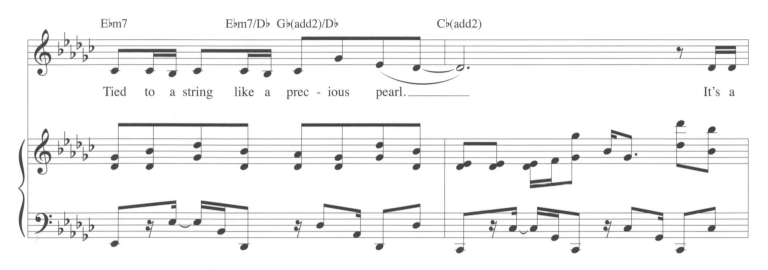

Tied to a string like a prec-ious pearl.___ It's a

pret-ty tight leash for a real-ly good girl.___

Good girl Win-nie Fos-ter ev-'ry day

62

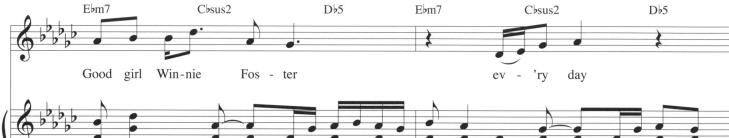

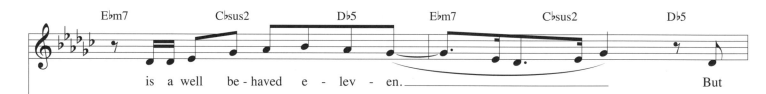

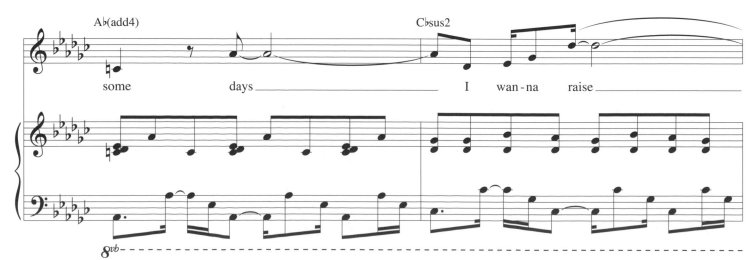

HOW TO USE HAL LEONARD ONLINE AUDIO

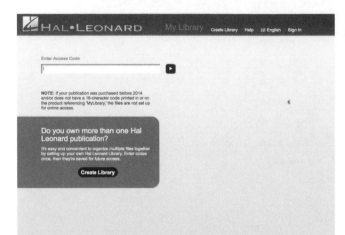

Because of the changing use of media, and the fact that fewer people are using CDs, we have made a shift to companion audio accessible online. In many cases, rather than a book with CD, we now have a book with an access code for online audio, including performances, accompaniments or diction lessons. Each copy of each book has a unique access code. We call this Hal Leonard created system "My Library." It's simple to use.

Go to www.halleonard.com/mylibrary and enter the unique access code found on page one of a relevant book/audio package.

The audio tracks can be streamed or downloaded. If you download the tracks on your computer, you can add the files to a CD or to your digital music library, and use them anywhere without being online. See below for comments about Apple and Android mobile devices.

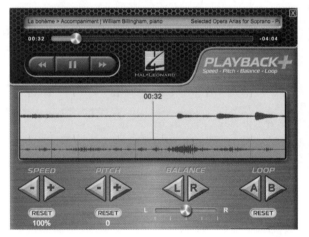

There are some great benefits to the My Library system. *Playback+* is exclusive to Hal Leonard, and when connected to the Internet with this multi-functional audio player you can:

• Change tempo without changing pitch
• Transpose to any key

Optionally, you can create a My Library account, and store all the companion audio you have purchased there. Access your account online at any time, from any device, by logging into your account at www.halleonard.com/mylibrary. Technical help may be found at www.halleonard.com/mylibrary/help/

Apple/iOS

Question: On my iPad and iPhone, the Download links just open another browser tab and play the track. How come this doesn't really download?

Answer: The Safari iOS browser will not allow you to download audio files directly in iTunes or other apps. There are several ways to work around this:

• You can download normally on your desktop computer, saving the files to iTunes. Then, you can sync your iOS device directly to your computer, or sync your iTunes content using an iCloud account.
• There are many third-party apps which allow you to download files from websites into the app's own file manager for easy retrieval and playback.

Android

Files are always downloaded to the same location, which is a folder usually called "Downloads" (this may vary slightly depending on what browser is used (Chrome, Firefox, etc)). Chrome uses a system app called "Downloads" where files can be accessed at any time. Firefox and some other browsers store downloaded files within a "Downloads" folder in the browser itself.

Recently-downloaded files can be accessed from the Notification bar; swiping down will show the downloaded files as a new "card", which you tap on to open. Opening a file depends on what apps are installed on the Android device. Audio files are opened in the device's default audio app. If a file type does not have a default app assigned to it, the Android system alerts the user.